This edition produced in **1993** for
Shooting Star Press Inc
230 Fifth Avenue
New York, NY 10001

Design: Rob Hillier, Andy Wilkinson
Editor: Jen Green
Drawings by Anthony Hodge
Illustrations by Ron Hayward Associates

The author, Anthony Hodge, is an artist
whose work is regularly exhibited. He has
taught art to adults and children for 20
years.

© Aladdin Books Ltd 1991

Created and produced by
Aladdin Books Ltd
28 Percy Street
London W1P 9FF

First published in 1991
in the United States by
Gloucester Press

ISBN 1-56924-023-X

Printed in Belgium

HANDS ON ARTS AND CRAFTS

DRAWING

Anthony Hodge

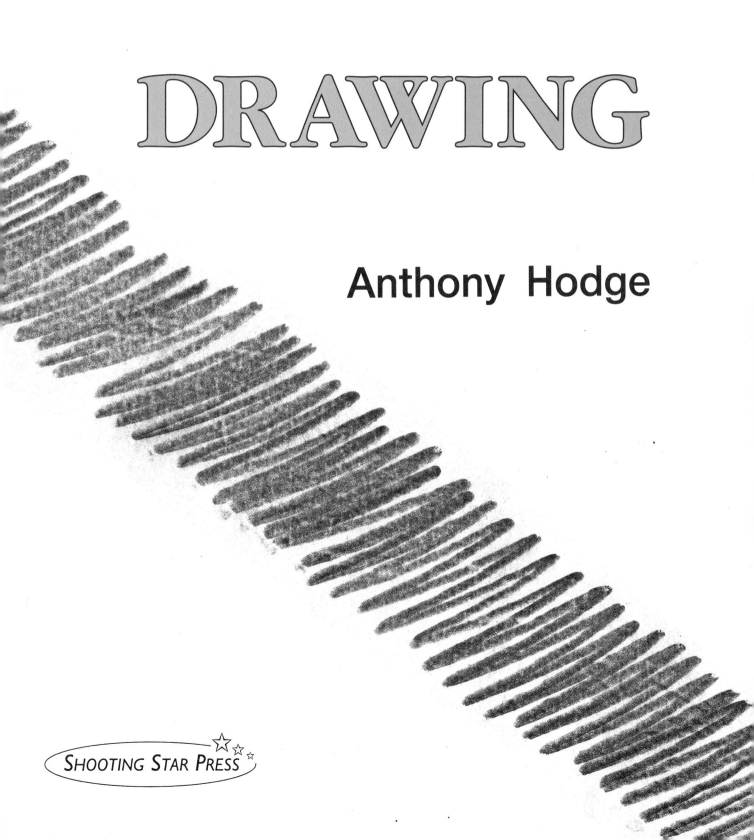

SHOOTING STAR PRESS

CONTENTS

INTRODUCTION

Drawing has a wonderful quality of immediacy, of something that is happening *now*. Its great advantage is that it can be done almost anywhere. With a sketch pad and pencil you need never be bored.

Starting with basics
This book aims to develop in you the natural talents and ideas that make every artist unique. We begin by examining the range of materials available. We look at some of the basic skills of drawing. Then these skills are used in a series of projects. We will explore sketching techniques and work up to more finished drawings. We will examine how simple forms can be developed into more complex ones such as the human figure. The main emphasis is on drawing what you see, but there are also projects that involve working from photographs and from your imagination.

Making connections
There are no hard and fast rules about how to draw, so try not to be too critical of your work. Drawing is about looking carefully and developing an understanding of what you see. It is an exhilarating way of feeling connected to the world.

▷ *"On the opposite page you can see some sketches I made at the zoo, using a black felt-tip pen. Whatever you feel about animals being kept in captivity, zoos are a wonderful place to draw."*

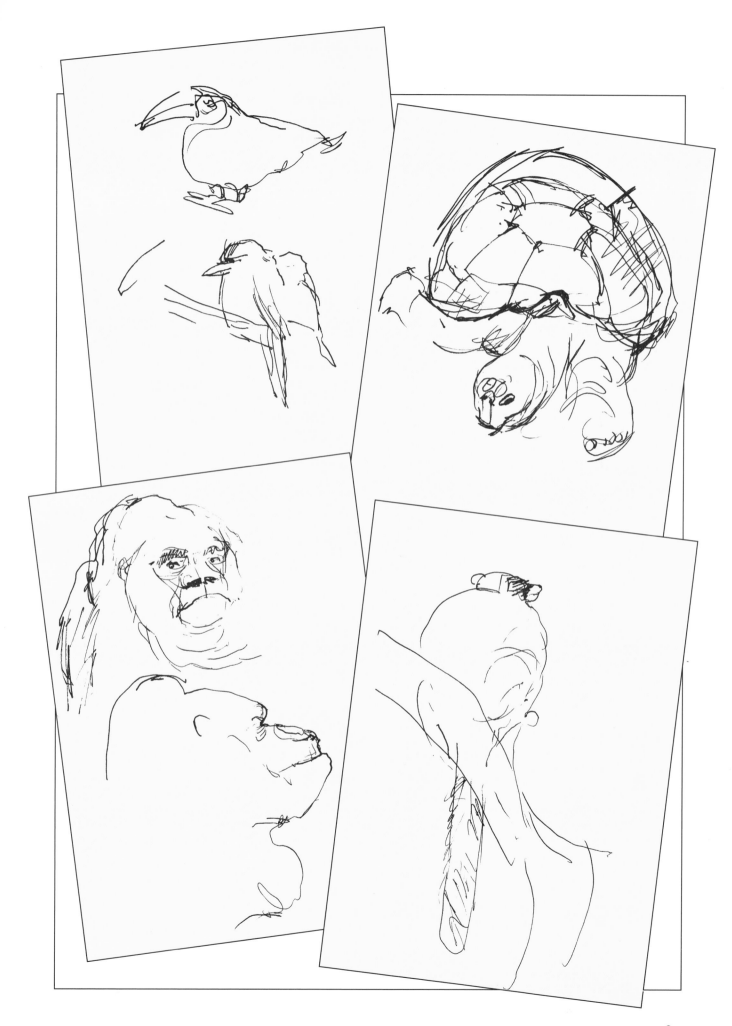

PENCIL, PEN AND WASH

Drawing involves making marks and there are plenty of different drawing tools you can use to do this. All drawing materials are made of particles of color, or *pigment*, bound together with a different kind of gum, or *medium*, to perform different jobs. These first pages are about getting to know the tools and experimenting with as many as possible.

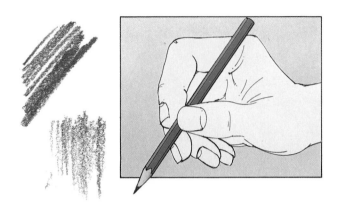

What feels most comfortable?
You will find some tools suit you more than others. Most people feel safer with a pencil than with a brush full of ink, as they feel they have less control with ink. Later on you may come to enjoy the hit and miss element of drawing with a brush, too.

Getting equipped
Gather together as many different kinds of mark-making tools as you can. It is not always necessary to buy expensive, new equipment. Keep a lookout for any unwanted bits and pieces that friends or relatives may have. The projects that appear later in this book are made in materials that are appropriate to the subject or style of the work. But there is no reason why you shouldn't use a different tool if you prefer, when you come to try them.

Pencils
Pencils are the basic drawing implement and you can produce all sorts of marks with a few pencils. Within the wooden tube of a pencil is the pigment, graphite, mixed with the medium, clay. Pencils are graded and numbered according to the hardness of the graphite. A graphite pencil marked HB is a good all-purpose tool. For a thicker, softer line, you can use anything from a 2B to a 6B.

4B

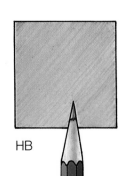

2B

HB

2H

4H

Pen and ink

India ink is a good, strong, black medium and can be used with a drawing pen, or fountain pen, or with a brush. Drawing pens can use many different nibs. A wide range of **felt-tip pens** is also on the market. Their range of expression is limited because the mark that they make is unvarying. Modern alternatives to the ink pen include the **Rotring pen**, used for technical drawing.

Pen and wash

To make a wash you need a brush that will hold plenty of ink and water. First make a drawing with pen and ink, and let it dry. There are two kinds of ink, permanent or waterproof ink, and nonwaterproof ink. If your drawing is in nonwaterproof ink, when you wet it again the lines will run. If your drawing is in permanent ink, the hard pen lines will contrast with the soft shadows of the wash.

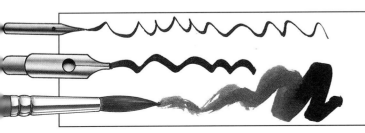

Nibs

Nibs for ink pens vary in size and thickness and, of course, the lines they make vary accordingly. Marks can also be made in ink with a paint brush.

CHARCOAL, CONTÉ AND CRAYON

Getting a grip

How you hold your drawing implement makes a big difference to the kind of line you produce. In general, if you hold your implement in the middle in a relaxed way, your arm muscles will relax, and the line you produce will be relaxed, too. If you hold your implement near the point, you can get harder, more intense marks. Try holding it at the end, to produce freer, looser marks.

Sharpening your pencils

Pencils and crayons can be sharpened with a pencil sharpener or with a sharp knife, preferably one with a safe, retractable blade. You can also use sandpaper to vary the point you get: a sharp point for thin, fine lines, and a flat edge for broad, thick lines.

Getting some support

Even if you buy your drawing paper in a pad, it may not be stiff enough to give you proper support by itself. You will need to rest your paper on a board of some kind. You can get one from an art store, or simply buy a piece of plywood or fiberboard from a hardware store.

Charcoal

Charcoal is made from burnt wood, usually willow, and is always black. It is available in sticks of various thicknesses, which are brittle and can tend to break. Charcoal is also available in *compressed* form, in a straight, hard stick, or in pencil form, encased in a paper cylinder that you can gradually tear away.

Fixative

Finished drawings, especially charcoal and pastel ones, need to be protected from smudging. This can be done by spraying them lightly with fixative.

Erasers

There are many different kinds of erasers. For chalk or charcoal drawing, it is best to use a kneaded eraser, a soft gray eraser that you can squeeze like clay into any shape you want.

Conté

Conté is a hard form of pastel compressed into a thin stick. It comes traditionally in black, white, and shades of brown, although other colors are now available. Drawing with brown rather than black conté can produce a softer, warmer drawing. Conté can be blended by rubbing it with your finger.

Wax crayon

Crayons are bold, simple sticks of color that come in many forms and prices. They can sometimes be dissolved with turpentine or mineral spirits, and applied with a brush or even with cotton. Used on a textured surface, crayons produce a grainy effect that can add considerable interest to your drawings.

What kind of paper?

Cartridge paper is fine for most pencil or ink drawings. Try out other kinds too, including colored paper. Textured paper is good for use with pastel, crayon and charcoal.

COLORED PENCIL AND PASTEL

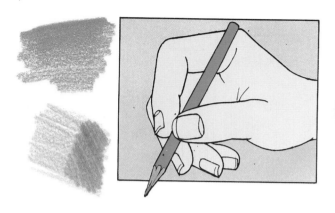

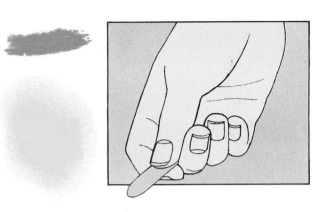

Colored pencils
Colored pencils are one of the most basic coloring tools. Many bright and wonderful colors are available. Artists like David Hockney frequently choose to use them. Although they are often used as colors in their own right, they mix and can be laid down on top of one another to achieve different effects.

Chalk pastels
Chalk pastels are pure pigment bound together with gum. They blend well if you rub them with your finger – this is messy, but effective. Pastel can be put on smoothly with the side of the chalk, or quite thickly if you press firmly with the end. As with most drawing materials, price and quality vary.

Colored pencil and wash
Water-soluble pencils are fun to experiment with. Lines drawn with them will blur to make an area of flat color if you lay a wash of clean water over them with a paint brush.

COLOR THEORY

The six colors you can see in the color wheel on the left are divided into two groups. Red, yellow and blue are called the *primary* colors. Orange, green and purple are the *secondary* colors, and are a mix of the two primaries on either side. In fact nearly all colors can be mixed from the primaries; some ways of mixing colors are shown below. The more colors are mixed together, the duller they become. The colors that are opposite each other on the color wheel are known as *complementaries*. When placed side by side, they bring out the best in each other. For example, red looks redder next to green, and vice versa.

△ *"Make a color wheel for yourself with the primary and secondary colors. Then try again, blending the secondaries from your primary colors."*

Colors can be mixed in various ways. In *cross-hatching*, shades of colored pencil are laid on top of each other.

Colors appear darker or lighter, depending on how hard you press down with your pencil or crayon.

Strokes of yellow wax crayon laid over blue produce a light green. Blue laid over yellow makes a darker green.

Wax crayons can be blended with a finger. If colors are rubbed too much, they will get dirty.

Felt-tip colors can be blended by over-lapping groups of tiny dots. This technique is used in color printing.

BASICS: LINE, TONE AND TEXTURE

"The artist," declared Picasso, "must find a way to convince people of the complete truth of his lies." Like a conjuror, the artist uses tricks to convince us of the reality of what he shows us. The next pages cover some of these basic tricks. Line, tone and texture are three of the most important.

Starting off
The project here is to try out line, tone and texture separately. Then you can combine them in a single drawing. Find a subject you want to explore using these three techniques. You may wish to work from a photograph of your pet or your favorite animal, perhaps.

Taking a line for a walk
Lines are used to describe the shape of objects. By varying the thickness of your lines you can show all that is necessary to capture your subject.

White paper is part of your picture
Notice how the different approaches affect the white paper that you are working on. In the line drawing, the lines enclose areas of white paper, which become shapes in their own right. In the tone drawing, much of the paper is covered with a tone of some kind. The areas of white represent the lightest tone. In the texture drawing, the white areas form an important contrast with the marks that cover the rest of the paper.

A lot can be left to the imagination, which can fill in what is missing.

Showing light and dark
The tone of an object is its darkness or lightness relative to other things. The cat in the middle picture below is darker than the rug, which is a lighter tone. But the tone of an object also changes depending on how light falls on it. Selective shading of parts of your drawing can be used to indicate these variations in tone, as shown in the picture top right.

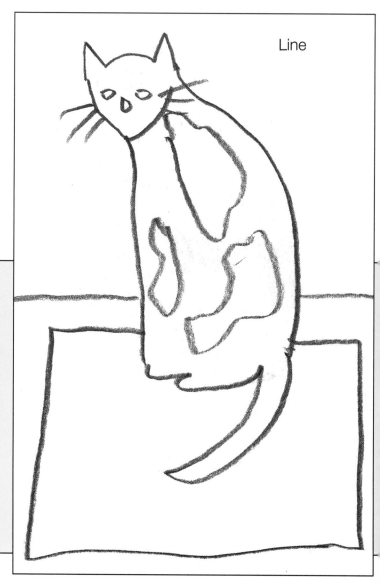

Line

What is it made of?

If your drawings have texture, they will be rich, varied, and exciting to look at. The texture of your pencils or crayons on rough paper also helps to convey the actual texture of your subject, like the hairiness of the cat or the coarseness of the rug in the picture bottom right.

"As you can see from my examples, the drawings for this project can be kept simple. It is not necessary to make your drawings complex, until you try in your final one (mine is top right) to combine all three techniques in a single image."

Tone

Texture

BASICS: FINDING THE FORM

An artist sometimes stalks his or her subject, moving in on it as gradually as a hunter moves in on his prey. It is not always possible to get things right the first time. Sometimes it is necessary to work in a very general way at first and only gradually approach the finished result.

Feeling your way

For this project, choose a simple object, such as a tin can or a box. Put it on the table in front of you and look at it carefully. Take a pencil and begin by sketching it loosely. Go over and over your drawing with very soft lines until the shape you want begins to appear. Be very free at this stage as all mistakes can be erased later. Gradually feel your way toward the finished drawing.

Drawing with X ray eyes

Try to think of your subject as transparent, so that you draw what you know to be there as well as what you can see. In the first drawing below, all of the bottom of the tin can is drawn in, although only part can be seen. At the second stage the form of the tin can becomes clearer. Tones begin to be indicated.

▷ *"The French painter Edgar Degas said that the artist does not draw what he sees, but what he must make others see. Try to bear this in mind when deciding which details to include in your drawing."*

Drawing to a conclusion

Once you have got the basic form more or less right, start to notice how the light falls on it and where shadows appear. The last stage can be done with a soft pencil which produces a dark line, with dark crayon, conté, or pastel, or with pen and ink. If you use pen and ink for the final drawing, you can rub out the pencil lines once the ink has dried.

Try different kinds of shading techniques to convey the texture and tone of your subject. Cross-hatching, dots, and lines running around the form can all help to convey the shape and character of your subject, as shown in the final drawing.

Practicing forms

Drawing can become second nature. The more you practice, the easier it becomes. Once you are familiar with this way of drawing, you can go on to do anything you like in the same way. Practice this method on other simple forms, like the ones that appear below. You can decide for yourself how much detail to put in.

Don't forget that sometimes you can overdraw. You will probably have to overwork a few drawings to find the right moment to stop. Remember that a fresh and lively drawing is often more interesting to look at than one that is overworked and labored.

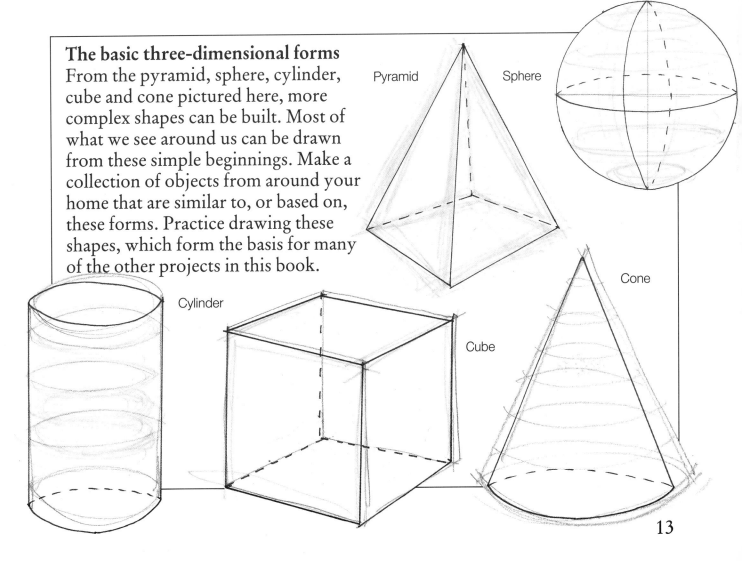

The basic three-dimensional forms

From the pyramid, sphere, cylinder, cube and cone pictured here, more complex shapes can be built. Most of what we see around us can be drawn from these simple beginnings. Make a collection of objects from around your home that are similar to, or based on, these forms. Practice drawing these shapes, which form the basis for many of the other projects in this book.

Pyramid

Sphere

Cylinder

Cube

Cone

BASICS: LIGHT AND SHADE

Imagine drawing a bowl of fruit and making it so lifelike that people feel hungry just looking at it! This may seem a tall order, but it is possible with a bit of practice to give your drawings a real depth and solidity. One of the keys to this is the use of light and shade.

When you were drawing the form on the previous page, you began to notice the play of light and shadow on it. Everything has a light and a dark side, and usually a part which is in between the two.

Throwing light on the subject

Take the subject of your previous project and a flashlight, or a lamp whose beam of light you can direct. Light up your object and study the shadows. You'll notice one shadow on the side of the object itself, making it look solid, and one that is the shadow cast by the object onto the surface on which it is standing.

Be a town planner

Most of what we see around us in the world is made up of simple shapes.

There is no light without shadow

Make a collection of objects based on the forms on the previous page. You might include a ball, a tin can and a box. Shine a light on them and practice seeing and drawing the forms with their shadows. Move your source of light around and watch the shadows change. The effects are demonstrated below in black and gray felt-tip pen. The gray areas show the middle or *half-tone*.

Although an object generally gets darker as less light falls on it, there is often a lighter part just before the outer edge. This is because light has bounced back from another surface (the table on which the objects have been placed, for example). It lights the object from behind. This is reflected light. With shiny objects, like glass or tin, light is reflected from many angles.

These may be built into complicated forms. Use your imagination and invent a picture in which the shapes come together. Imagine you have been asked to design a new town. Think of all the shapes of buildings you could design using the basic forms. What kind of vehicles can you picture driving through the streets?

Where is your sun?
Draw in the outlines of your forms first. Then decide where the sun is (it may not actually appear in your drawing, but the effects of it will). The position of the sun determines where the shadows fall and how long they are. As the sun goes down, shadows get longer. When you have finished, look and see how real buildings in sunlight compare with the ones you have drawn. Yours may be better designed!

▽ *"In my felt-tip drawing the sun appears quite low in the sky, and casts long shadows. Windows and other details can make your sketch more interesting."*

BASICS: PERSPECTIVE

Perspective is a means of creating a feeling of space in your drawings. It is a way of trying to represent the three-dimensional world on a flat piece of paper. To achieve this sense of space, you must establish the proper place on paper for things that are close to you and those that are far away. Things that are near must appear to advance toward you on paper, and things that are further away should be seen to go back, or *recede*, in your drawing, too.

Do we need rules?
Several hundred years ago in Italy, artists laid down a set of rules they felt helped to show perspective. Today some artists understand these rules and make use of them. Some understand the rules and choose not to use them; others get by without knowing about them at all. The rules are given here so that you can understand them and then decide whether or not you want to use them.

A great deal has been written about the theory of perspective. But the best way of practicing it is to observe your surroundings carefully and put down on paper the things you notice.

Three techniques
In drawing there are three main techniques for showing perspective. They appear in the main picture and are described on the opposite page. Get to know and practice each of them separately before trying the project, which is to put them together in a more complex picture. Some subjects are more suited to one technique than another.

▷ *"My main drawing shows the three techniques in combination. The figures show the technique of overlapping. The street is shown to recede into the background through the use of linear perspective. Tones and textures are more pronounced in the foreground, so this area looks closest to us."*

Linear

Overlapping

Tonal

The secrets of perspective

The examples on the left show the three main ways of showing perspective. The first is linear perspective. In this technique, lines that in fact run parallel to one another appear to meet on a point on the horizon known as vanishing point.

The second detail demonstrates the technique of overlapping. When one object is in front of another, the object in front hides part of the one behind. Test out this theory by looking around you and making drawings of your own.

The third technique is tonal perspective. Strong, dark marks will separate the front or foreground of a drawing from the softer lines of the background. So differences in tone can make parts of a drawing seem closer or further away.

BASICS: COMPOSITION

There is something to be said for the idea of making drawings of things as you find them. Composition, however, is about rearranging things and ordering them in a new way that seems more balanced and harmonious. In this project you can test this out for yourself.

The artist Paul Cézanne used to spend hours setting up his still-life subjects, even using coins to tip up bowls and jars so he could see inside more easily. By the time he had started work on a picture, he had practically finished! His subject already looked exactly as he wanted it to in the final work. How did he know what he wanted?

What feels right for you?
A good feel for composition can be developed by creating your own picture by trial and error. Make a collection of household objects.

Which way up?
Your drawing paper has a particular shape. You can, of course, decide which way up to hold it, making a picture that is wide or tall. Before you begin, spend some time imagining how each arrangement will look on paper.

A composition is a group of colored shapes in certain positions. Try some unlikely ones, even those that you know will look peculiar. Experiment with a series of arrangements on a tabletop or even on the floor. Try out compositions that you think will look unbalanced in some way: top-heavy, cramped, or too spaced out, as well as ones that look balanced. Unorthodox compositions sometimes produce good results.

Choose ones you feel might go well together in a picture. In the examples below there are five, but you might like to start with more. You could then discard some as you go along, if you find they don't fit in.

Trying out composition
Rearrange your objects and make a series of drawings based on them. Test out the idea that a harmonious or pleasing composition is a balanced one. In a balanced composition, a single large object can appear to equal two smaller ones. Perhaps you could have one or more of the objects only partially in your picture. Many artists have used this technique deliberately, to make unexpected compositions.

▽ *"Compositions can look orderly, comfortable, or plain crazy! My three examples here are quite sensible, but you don't have to be!"*

DRAWING THE HEAD

Our faces tell a lot about who we are and how we are feeling, whether we like it or not. Over the next pages we will examine how to draw them step by step, looking at the proportions of the head, the features, and finally, how to achieve a likeness.

The shape of the head

Viewed from the front, the head is an egg-shaped form sitting on the cylinder of the neck. From the side, it is helpful to see the head as two overlapping eggs, and the three-quarter view is the same, only with the second egg more hidden. These views are illustrated below. Practice drawing the shape of the head and positioning the features within it as described in the box below. Use the method described on pages 12-13 to feel your way toward the form and proportions of the head.

A study from life

When you are confident that you can manage these proportions, ask a friend to sit for you. Perhaps you can draw each other at the same time; or you may prefer to try a self-portrait. Make drawings of your subject's head from side, front and three-quarter views. Don't worry about getting a perfect likeness at this stage.

▷ *"My simple line drawing could be taken further by adding shading, but I felt it might become confused. Sometimes it's best to quit while you are ahead, rather than risk going on for too long."*

Making the headlines

The proportions of the head are shown here. The first thing to notice is that the eyes come halfway down the head, and not higher up. The end of the nose lies midway between eyes and chin; the mouth comes halfway between nose and chin. There is the width of an eye between the eyes, and also across the bottom of the nose. On the sides of the head, the ears should be placed midway between the eyes and the nose.

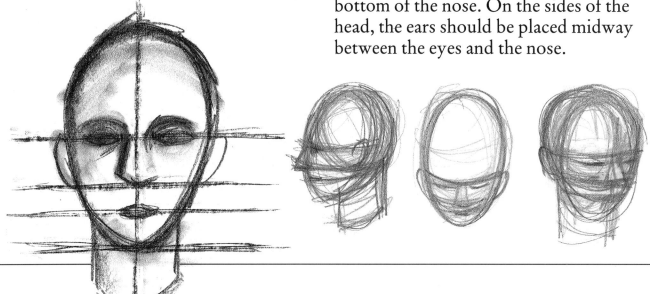

21

FEATURES AND EXPRESSIONS

We all have in common two eyes and ears, a nose, and a mouth. These features may conform to certain shapes: the nose is a triangular form, eyes are oval in shape. But no two people's features are ever exactly the same, even if they are related.

On the opposite page, the different features are drawn step by step. The first drawing in each sequence shows the basic form. The second shows the individual character developing, and in the third, shadow has been added to emphasize the form.

A subject for your portrait
When you are familiar with drawing features and expressions, it's time to try to achieve a likeness. This is fun as long as no one minds whether you succeed or not. When Oliver Cromwell had his portrait painted, he insisted that he was shown "warts and all." The artist was lucky on this occasion, as people can be sensitive about how they look! If you find it difficult to get someone to pose, try drawing from a photograph of someone you know or admire.

Getting a likeness
A likeness depends on drawing the features and capturing how they combine together. The rest of the face is almost as important as the features. The distance between the eyes, or the gap between nose and mouth, vary as much as the shape of the nose. In a portrait it's important to get these details right.

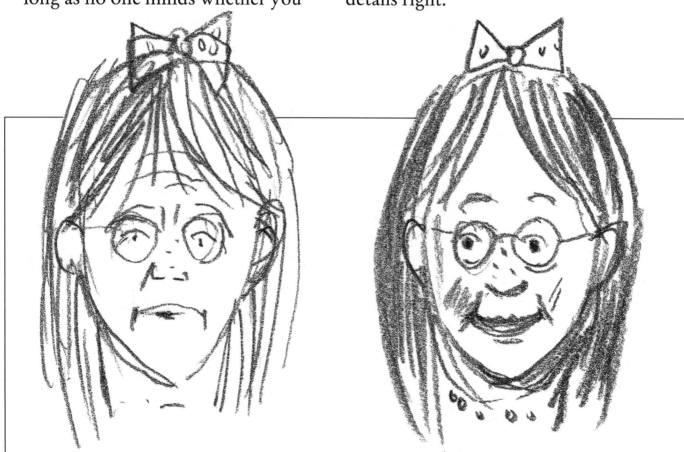

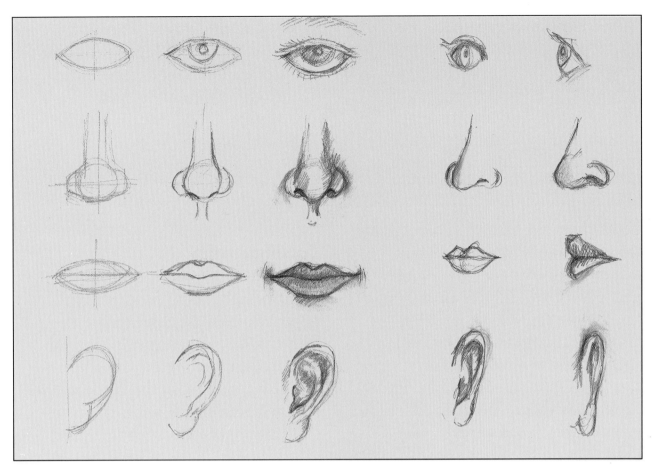

△ *"Above I have sketched front, side and three-quarter views of the same features. Cross-hatching has added solidity."*

Putting on expressions

The drawings on the left show the subject of the previous page in different moods: first sad, then happy, and finally just puzzled. The features and even the hair droop downward in the sad face, as if there is no energy to keep them up. Enthusiasm lifts the lines upward in the happy face. In a puzzled face, the lines are undecided and waver in different directions. Try out these expressions yourself in a mirror and feel how the muscles in your face move. See how your face changes as you practice looking delighted, annoyed or tired.

THE HUMAN FIGURE

When the American space program launched the rocket *Pioneer 10* into outer space, they attached a plaque to inform extraterrestrials about the planet earth. The plaque featured a drawing of two figures – a man and a woman. It's strange to think that other beings might look very different to us. Imagine that you've been given the task of showing aliens what humans look like. For an accurate picture you will need to show the body in proportion.

Getting things in proportion

Proportion is about comparing the size of one thing to another. For the artist, it is about showing different sizes correctly on paper. The drawings on the right show the proportions of the human figure. The length of the body is often measured in relation to the head. The average adult, whether male or female, is seven heads tall. The torso is three heads long from the chin to the top of the legs, and divides into thirds at the nipple line and navel. The distance from the top of the legs to the soles of the feet also measures three heads. Children's heads are larger in proportion to the rest of their bodies. Adult or child, with your arms stretched out sideways, the distance between your fingertips measures the same as your height – try it!

Foreshortening

Here the story gets more complicated; these proportions appear to change as we move about. Parts of the body appear larger or smaller, depending on whether they are near or far from the person looking at them. We found out about this in the project on perspective.

If someone's leg or arm is pointing directly at you, part of its length will be hidden. This is known as *foreshortening*. You can see it on the right in the drawings of the figures sitting and crouching, and also in the sketches at the bottom of the opposite page.

Practicing foreshortening

Foreshortening takes a more dramatic turn when you look at the figure from an unusual angle. As shown in the drawings left and middle opposite, a person with his arm outstretched toward you, or lying down, will seem to have an enormous hand or enormous feet. Have a go at drawing someone in these positions. It takes a lot of practice to get these things to look right, but you can have fun on the way as long as you don't mind making mistakes. The third picture is a sketch of the artist looking down at his own body and drawing himself at work. Try it. If you shut one eye, you can even see your nose, and include it in the picture, as he did.

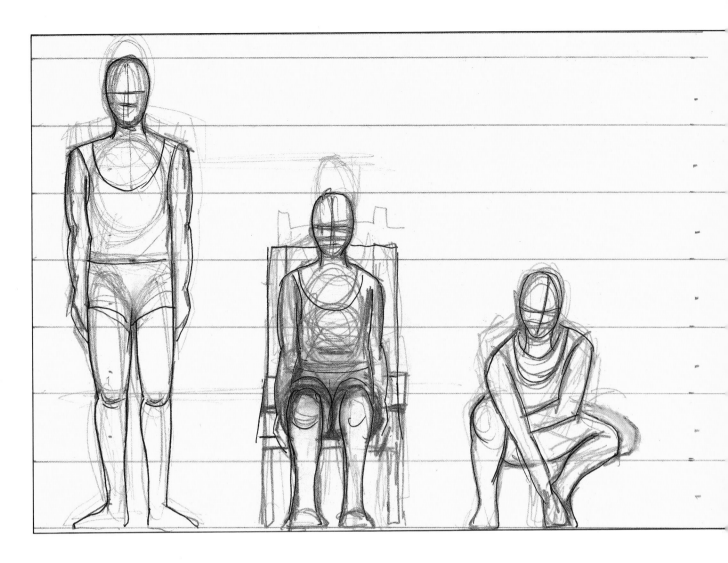

△ "Above I have drawn the proportions of the standing figure. You might want to copy this first. Try it again from memory, and then check the measurements against a real person."

△ "The seated figure shows how two heads have been 'lost' from the height; the space from hips to knees has become foreshortened. Again, check this against the real thing."

△ "The crouching figure is more complicated, as the top half is also foreshortened as it leans toward you. The legs are foreshortened differently. Can you see how?"

PEOPLE ON THE MOVE

"Don't try to run before you can walk," the saying goes, and it's true that if you overreach yourself in the real world, you fall and hurt yourself. However, in a world of flat paper, if we take a risk that doesn't come off, we are none the worse for it.

A sense of balance

You can learn a lot about how the figure moves by trying it yourself! As you walk or run, practice being aware of what happens to your body. Feel how the weight shifts from one leg to the other, so that each leg in turn holds the body up as the other swings forward to take the next step. Try squatting down and feel how your weight is distributed.

Let's get moving

We take walking and running for granted, but we all had to learn how to balance. The illustrations below show a figure running. Each part of the sequence flows into the next.

Notice how at each stage, the running figure is balanced by the different positions of the limbs.

The project takes this idea further. Find a photograph of someone running, an athlete perhaps, in a newspaper or magazine. Photographs can be confusing, so choose one where you can really see what's happening. Make a drawing based on the photograph you have chosen.

Before and after

Before photographs were invented, artists had to rely on their eyes and their imagination. The next step is to try to imagine the positions the runner would be in before and after the photograph was taken. Make sketches of these positions on either side of your first drawing.

Having finished the project, try drawing people on the move around you. Get used to working quickly and you will be surprised how your drawing can improve.

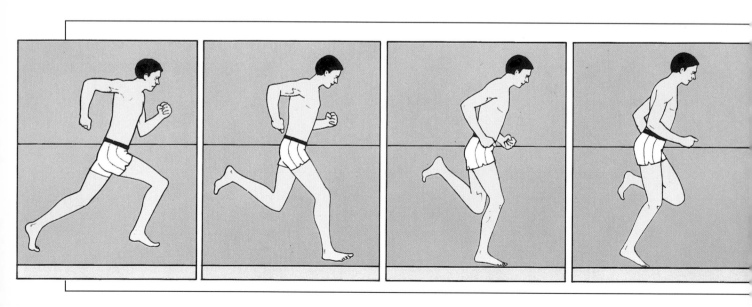

△ *"Here is an example of this project with my attempts at guessing 'before and after' positions for my runner. I've tried to get a feeling of energy and movement into the drawings so that, unlike the photograph I drew from, my sketches aren't frozen and still. Try it yourself and see how well you can do!"*

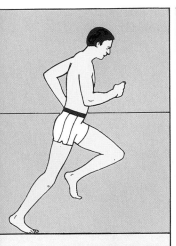
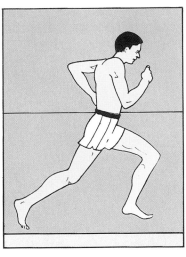

A man on the run

The illustrations of the running man are included for information, rather than as examples of how you should draw. They give a clear explanation of what happens when we run. However, your drawings should try to convey not only information, but a sense of movement too. Try making your pencil move across the paper enthusiastically, to show the runner's energy.

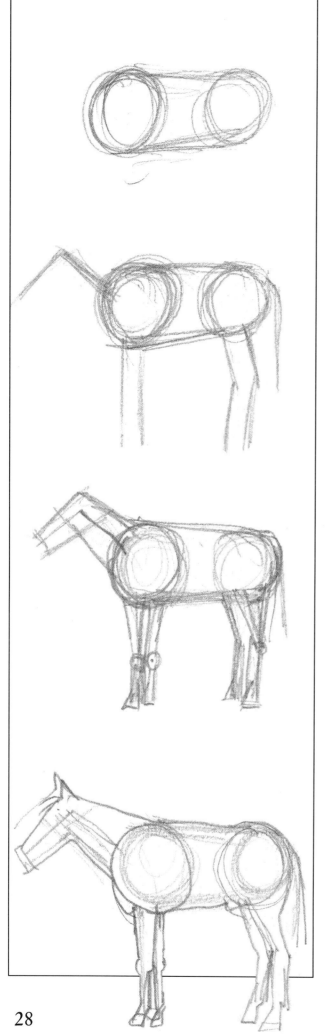

ANIMAL STUDIES

The variety in the world of nature provides a constant source of wonder and excitement to the artist. From camels to crocodiles, from bats to bulls, animals provide a wonderful opportunity to experiment with lines and mark-making.

The texture of an animal's coat is particularly important. Let your eyes enjoy the softness of cats, the roughness of dogs, the sleekness of horses, and the prickliness of porcupines.

Back to basics
"Treat nature by means of the cylinder, sphere and cone," said the artist Paul Cézanne.

◁ *"In this example you can see how a drawing can 'evolve,' or be built up gradually. The basic shapes develop step by step into a particular horse. At each stage, more detail is added until, finally, the animal has its own special presence. Make your own version of this sequence of drawings all in one go. You might want to put the figure of a rider on the horse's back to make your drawing more interesting."*

▽ *"In the final stages, I added tone to make my horse look more solid and to complete my picture."*

The simple shapes we studied earlier are the basis for animal forms, and can be used to make your drawings look convincing. The drawings on the left show how the figure of a horse evolves from a few basic shapes. Try this out with your own drawing and then try a similar method with other animals. What basic shapes might develop into a cow, a dog or a cat?

Animals don't stay still
What all living creatures have in common is that they move and won't pose for you. As with a moving human figure, however, the combination of photographs, your

imagination and, most important, your eyes, can work very well.

Field studies
Don't be afraid to draw from real life whenever possible. Even if your drawing doesn't have a textbook likeness, it may well have a special quality about it. There is nothing so exciting for the artist as confronting the real thing armed only with a pencil and pad. Use a rough sketch book; the less expensive the better, so you will not feel that what you do has to be perfect. Learn to draw quickly and directly, and your pictures will take on a life of their own.

Caught on the hop
Below you can see an example of how an animal moves. When drawing animals in motion, it is important to let your subject draw itself for you. Look at the animal and allow your pencil to follow the forms in front of you without looking at the paper.

Make a sequence of drawings as the animal moves. When it changes position, don't be frustrated. Keep the same drawing going if it is only a slight change. If your subject changes into a different pose entirely, begin another drawing. Return to the previous one when the original pose is taken up again.

PRESENTATION

Finished drawings, particularly ones in charcoal, conté or pastel, should be sprayed with fixative to protect them and prevent them from smudging. Use fixative in a well ventilated room and be careful not to get any in your eyes. Try to spray your drawing as evenly as possible.

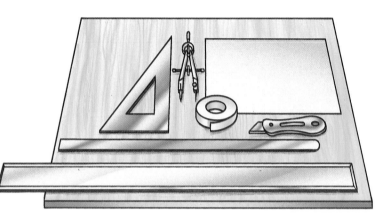

For the record
Keep a record of when your drawings were made by putting the date on them, and possibly also the place where they were made. One day you will look back with interest and notice how your work has changed over the years.

Mounting your work
Mats play an important part in the presentation process. Mounting your drawings can make them look better than you ever thought possible. In general, steer away from brightly colored mats; white and cream mats are usually effective. Measure the area for your mat accurately with a ruler, and cut it out carefully with a knife.

Drawing with a mat
Mats can also be used in the drawing process itself if you are using brush and ink, or if you are working very freely with any material. Before you begin, place a mat on your paper, framing the area in which you intend to draw. Allow your drawing to go over the edges of the mat. When you have finished, remove the mat. You will find a clean edge framing your work which will make it look smart.

PRACTICAL TIPS

Keeping equipment safe

Protecting your drawing equipment is important. Keep your paper, pencils and drawing pads together in one place. This will help from a practical point of view, and give you a feeling of continuity in your work. Keep your paper in a drawer where it can lie flat and will not get creased or soiled.

Drawing large and free

Try drawing on a large scale. Don't feel that your work has to be small and detailed. You may find that you are able to express yourself more completely if you can move your arm freely. If you are the sort of person who likes working on large drawings, you may find it easier to draw standing up at an easel. Art stores stock these in various shapes and sizes. There is also a piece of equipment called a horse, which enables you to sit and work at a drawing board at the same time.

More about paper

There are many different kinds of paper, from newsprint to handmade paper. Experiment with as many sorts as possible, but don't feel you have to rely on expensive equipment all the time. The French artist Pierre Bonnard used to do most of his drawings on the backs of old envelopes! Expensive equipment can sometimes inhibit you from working freely.

Watercolor paper has a texture which is fun to work on, particularly in pastel, conté, crayon or charcoal. Its rough surface will make your strokes look broken and bold. Charcoal paper has a delicate ribbed surface.

It allows you to blend your strokes and create velvety tones.

Drawing with an eraser

An eraser can also be used as a drawing tool in its own right. It is used to introduce highlights into areas of dark tone. Try this for yourself: shade in an area of your paper with pencil or charcoal. Then draw with your eraser and reveal the white paper again. You have effectively drawn in the areas you would usually leave out. If your eraser gets dirty, rub it clean on a spare scrap of paper.

Drawing outside

Drawing outdoors can be very rewarding, but presents its own set of problems. You need to find a comfortable spot to sit, from where your subject is clearly visible. If your position becomes too cramped, your drawing is likely to suffer. If it is windy you will need to tape your paper down, or restrain it with clips. If your paper is in direct sunlight, its brightness may dazzle you. Hold your sketch pad so that your page is in the shade.

Getting ideas

Keep a scrapbook of images cut from newspapers and magazines as possible subject matter for future work.

Visit art galleries whenever you can, and learn from the work displayed there. A great deal about cross-hatching and other techniques can be learned from etchings in museums. Carry a pocket-size sketch book around with you for noting down ideas, and making quick sketches for later use.

INDEX

▽ *"This picture of a stormy day shows the range of marks that can be made using the materials described in this book: pen and ink, pencil, conté, and pastel."*